Hymns from the Sisters

Dear Same Trina,
enjoy the Yorkshire
Landscape!

with love

good wishes!

Emma

HYMNS FROM THE SISTERS

EMMA CONALLY-BARKLEM

QUERENCIA PRESS

© Copyright 2023
Emma Conally-Barklem

All Rights Reserved

ISBN 978 1 959118 68 8

Unaltered cover photo "Moorland Landscape" by Charlotte Christie
Digitally manipulated by Emily Perkovich

.

www.querenciapress.com

First Published in 2023

Querencia Press, LLC
Chicago IL

Printed & Bound in the United States of America

ALSO BY EMMA CONALLY-BARKLEM

THE RIDINGS

"*Hymns from the Sisters* by Emma Conally-Barklem is a captivating collection of poetry that pays homage to the Brontë sisters, delving into their lives and their profound influence on literature. Conally-Barklem's deep admiration is evident in every carefully crafted verse, offering readers a glimpse into the intertwined worlds of Charlotte, Emily, and Anne Brontë.

One of the standout poems for me in this collection is *Fencers*, a poignant insight into Charlotte Brontë's grief and solitude following the devastating loss of her sisters, Emily and Anne. Conally-Barklem's words masterfully capture Charlotte's profound sense of loss and the sisters' deep bond as they wove their literary tapestries side by side. Readers can feel the weight of Charlotte's sorrow through this poem and understand how the collaborative writing process shaped the sisters' lives.

Throughout the collection, it becomes apparent that Conally-Barklem possesses a deep understanding of the sisters and the environment in which they lived. Her intimate connection to the area shines through, infusing the poems with a sense of authenticity and grounding them in the landscape that shaped the Brontës' lives and works. This adds an extra layer of depth to the collection, immersing readers in the world of the Brontë sisters and their creative endeavours.

As a reader, I found myself eagerly turning the pages to uncover the next poem, each one offering a unique perspective on the lives and minds of the Brontë sisters. Conally-Barklem's passion for her subject matter is palpable, breathing life into their stories and allowing readers to connect with these literary icons more personally.

In conclusion, *Hymns from the Sisters* by Emma Conally-Barklem is a moving and heartfelt collection of poetry that admirably encapsulates the lives of the Brontë sisters based on places, objects, and events. With a keen eye for detail and a profound understanding of her subjects, Conally-Barklem has created a work that honours the sisters' legacy while offering readers a fresh perspective on their lives. Poems like *Fencers* and *Hair* are particularly captivating, showcasing the author's ability to blend historical context, emotional resonance, and the magic of poetry. If you are a fan of the Brontë or appreciate beautifully crafted verse, this book is a must-read."

—Kate Benson, *The Brontë Sisters* UK

"Emma Conally-Barklem is a poet with a love of the works of the Brontë sisters and strong links to the village they spent most of their lives in—Haworth in West Yorkshire. Her latest release is Hymns from the Sisters, a book of poetry that celebrates not only her love of the Brontë sisters' works but also her experience of growing up in a place so steeped in their legacy it is known fondly as Brontë country.

The collection is comprised of nineteen poems covering many aspects of the family's lives and works including those inspired by well-known anecdotes from the sisters' childhood, Branwell's troubles, Anne's death in Scarborough, Charlotte's dislike of her pupils, and a lock of Emily's beautiful hair. These poems will strike a chord with admirers and devotees of the Brontës (myself included) who like Conally-Barklem also feel a close connection with this remarkable family despite the centuries separating them. The poems capture the essence of the sisters and all we know about them as well as the enduring fascination with their words and the much-loved and magnificent works of fiction and poetry they produced and published against the odds.

Conally-Barklem's collection overflows with tenderness for the Brontë family, her knowledge of their lives and works, and her own experience of being inspired by this remarkable family. If a hymn is a form of thanksgiving and a poem is the expression of feelings, the two combine in this collection to produce a beautiful, moving, and sometimes quirky lovesong to one woman's relationship and journey with those brilliant Brontës. Reader, I loved it."

—Nicola Friar, author of *A Tale of Two Glass Towns*, editor, & blogger

CONTENTS

Introduction

My personal history is rooted in The Brontë Parsonage and Haworth. Top Withins, Penistone moor, and the Brontë waterfall are all a part of my childhood. Since I was a little girl, my mum, grandma, and I took the Oakworth bus from Fairweather Green to visit. Then later, my mum drove us until it was just us. Recently, I drove us until it was just me. Three became one in the same way the pacing and reading of the Brontë sisters around the dining room table dwindled to one pair of footsteps. I am left to keep the home fires burning. A fire lit with joy and wonder at the temporality of life and the timelessness of books.

A Brontë foot would fit clean in my hand. Their tiny waists startle anybody familiar with Yorkshire portions. These meagre shells contained a vastness of spirit. Their blend of frailty and toughness I know from my own humble beginnings near Thornton village. It takes a lot to dream your way out of a place. The Brontës knew that vulnerability is a type of strength. Open chambered words, defiance, an Indian scarf, an aversion to strangers, the moor and curlew cries running through their veins. Their lives, the minutiae of their domestic arrangements, their raiment chimes a fascination, difficult to explain, but felt. The Brontë sisters shot many arrows of truth from their Yorkshire version of an ivory tower. Like Patrick Brontë discharging his pistol into the stonemasonry of St Michael and All Angels church, their arrows were audacious and rebellious. The Brontë sisters knew that to flout convention and expectations was both delicious and freeing.

A writer reminds us that the world is up for disruption.

This collection is a summation of all that The Brontës have meant to me in terms of their literature, their lives, their historical and social significance, and their legacy as a lifelong connection between myself and my mother. Battered photo albums are filled with winter walks, days out, and picnics with my Jamaican dad and Yorkshire mother as my brother and I grew up around purple heather and under lowering skies.

This collection is for all that is lost and all that remains.

It is especially for my mother.

—Emma Conally-Barklem

Rupture

—Inspired by the story Patrick Brontë, father of the Brontë sisters, told about his son Branwell and two youngest daughters, Emily and Anne, being caught up in the Crow Hill explosion of 1824. Emily was just six at the time.

I didn't bleed because the red already darned my soul

I could have cried out

Clawed earthbog under my nails and straifed the pit impaling worms like a Kittiwake

But, I stopped.

Plumdense the roseated falcon who sank longing into valour

Her eye's lens a portal.

So, I just could not will this into being, a catastrophic event that smacked of fear!

Not with the thrill of inert gases shifting around my ears—

Silk shoes squelched in the moor's rupture is all and I

in rapture—

I kept it close, this explosion

Returned pious-seeming as a sexton and picked grit from my crossed tooth.

Oafs & Asses

—Inspired by Charlotte Brontë's description of the pupils she taught for three years at Roe Head School.

Oafs and asses stop me writing with their doltish scrawl of pluperfect subjunctives & spilt infinitives,

My head is splintered away from Zamorna with his charismatic whiskers & powdered blue eye,

To sniffing chits & clicking boots,

My roots call me back through Luddendenfoot & galloping brook to the hills that will hold my name.

Now, I am tamed, riven peculiar by shrill squawks & spurious bells which knell my fury & quell the extraordinary,

burrs of lurid lurching words which fork the insipid scurry to learn,

Hooked to a system of maiden aunts who comb me free of liberty.

A Don't Like Strangers
—after Emily Brontë

A don't like strangers, temporal and petty

Not like exploding hillsides, surly skies and tinkling waterfall sewn into rooks of rough-hewn existence

Even things grown off the earth are preferable to people.

A can pilla potato and smell that dung bitter fug from whence it sprang

The dog knows

Senses my animal

Petticoats and laces are immaterial to that what's real.

Real yet indifferent

A turning wheel of seasons that leak through ma shoes

Remind me this soul can be called home, summoned back at any time

So, leave me alone.

To moan and not yet see who I am in this pricked out existence when really

I span lifetimes...slabs of stone

Comfort those

That are passing through

Strung out satellites

More blood than bone

He

—Inspired by a viewing of a portrait of Anne Brontë in the private collection of the Brontë Parsonage Museum. Anne's facial expression is intriguing. The poem reflects on her brother's physical and mental decline and the subsequent writing of 'The Tenant of Wildfell Hall.'

He

carried my mother's name all the way from Penzance. Clean, monied, upright, distinct smacking of Georgian parlours and honourable rank. He

sunk our purse in misdeeds, avarice, and opiates, how to cope when this fiendish one writhes, befuddled, insensate. My

cheek may speak pink and white, the red campion of my portrait mouth upturns, a furrow in my brow as I turn to stonemasonry, carving out your legacy, chip chip, I

gouge paper like stone to tell this tale of debauchery gone sour. Who

would believe from my tightly wound curls and glacial stare that I'd let the curls down and press the point of your sorrow underneath this wretched bear I

call brother?

Fencers

> —*The Brontë sisters had a habit of walking around their dining room table discussing their ideas and writing. After the deaths of Emily and Anne, Charlotte kept up the tradition.*

Like fencers, we tilt and parry, *Allez!*

Emily makes a jab, I interject, *touché*!

Anne giggles, turns around the drop-leaf table,

A veritable hurricane of thoughts and ideas sail in like jonquils around a locum of ink blots, candle burn and carved E as *she* leaves a trace which cannot be erased.

Sarcastic riposte turns into a feint,

Hushed now, Anne quietly enunciates ecumenical verses from our mother's hand,

The game is up, solo promenade, my sisters turned sylph, I match my foot to their tracks 'til the clock strikes eleven and they melt en plein air

Ellen

—Inspired by a description in Claire Harman's stellar biography 'Charlotte Brontë: A Life' which implies that Charlotte would have been happy keeping house with her lifelong friend Ellen Nussey rather than Ellen's brother who proposed to her.

It was your brother who asked, but I would it 'twere you.

Whose sweet enigmatic face I kept pressed in tissue

          around the furious Belgian who entranced but did not

 keep my stoppered up forlornities.

A quieter passion

that may have sent you (an inconstant streamer) to ponder an eventual revulsion

with no other ear I could not stop the glottal loneliness that limed my lips but set ink soaring crazed kite zig zag, on a rack of copy books and conjugations.

Your sealing wax had a particular aroma

though seldom and rare would it press flat the worry between my eyes,

      still it did come,

An iced sugar branding of your banal seeings and tendings which seemed exotically peopled with advent and stimuli

whilst I drew up a fortress against the sensual idolaters who passed as benign schoolgirls and tore shavings & sheaths out,

stabbed each star corner

 to a mast that was cloven.

The distance a rivet to your peony attention

a flower I would have courted

with another face,

in another time.

The Lady Saved from the Waves

—Inspired by Patrick Brontë's burning of his wife, Maria's volumes of 'The Lady' magazine, a great loss to her children who had precious few of their mother's belongings. An added irony is that they had survived being shipwrecked in the Atlantic and were considered important enough to be saved.

I heard he burnt them, romantic trifles

Saline-flowered from a stormy Atlantic crossing

Water-marked bullion treasure of how to write, fairer sex not withstanding

A mother's maiden voyage, buoyant, fragrant as cornflowers 'til corrugated and hollowed, all she could call for was a Cornish setting of the fire, a pyre of her broken hopes, tug-boat from Thornton, memento mori up in smoke,

He broke the ocean pact, a pax on his fury that swallowed up in puerile worry, her drowned sketches,

of how to be a lady.

Enigma

—Inspired by a viewing of Emily Brontë's account book as part of the private collection at The Brontë Parsonage Museum. It is seldom displayed but intrigues academics and researchers alike with its cut-out pages.

Page edges are marbled,

   onyx oblong, banal

      you search for my traces in torn off stubs,

         cut short, obtuse, self-effaced, debased,

            racing towards the otherworld, a slippage in time allows your hands to hold mine,

            where mine have been between two hundred years

         Slender but strong enough to pummel Keeper

And winch myself around deadening furniture as my lungs gave out,

Can you glean my nature from your salt-spiked fingers which linger grasping through ink dim mahogany shelves   my lips curl at your folly,

trying to breathe, a clockwork bellows animation into my objects

so I may rise,

necromancer, Minerva, Lazarus, on the cusp of existence, summoned

thus to answer your very many many many questions

Weightman

—After William Weightman, believed to have been in love with and loved by Anne Brontë before his tragic, untimely death from cholera contracted during a pastoral visit to a young girl in the parish.

I'd had my notions from the Duke of Wellington about a well-heeled, sincere gentleman with perfumed gloves and chivalrous élan

Not a passing curate with soft cheeks who would prate mildly every Sunday so I'd feel the weight of the man through *Acts and Epistles*, the sum of him sighed through the vestry where the devil himself is decried.

Mildness belies the crushed gooseberry tartness of our eyes as they smart from overfeeling regard

Hard done by, his piety tore a hole through my hopes, too soon,

His youthed looks brooked vanity, unjust, my book spoked my love for posterity

A whisper gone, in a whisper gone!

The jar of preserves stood dusty on the shelf as she who smote him followed thereafter.

Scarborough

*—Inspired by Charlotte Brontë's moccasins which she took to
Scarborough after the death of her sister Anne. They are now displayed
in the Brontë Parsonage Museum.*

Deerskin, beaded, she packed them up and broke them in amidst the
breakers of Scarborough beach, her eyes stretched far from North Sea
to Atlantic, the Cornish bream in her veins, but nothing clement here,
just the stolen exoticism of Mohawk moccasins from warmer climes to
Leven the cold hoar frost of loss.

Homely

— "Homely-faced creature! She wants some Tomkins or another to love her and be in love with" William Makepeace Thackeray in his letters about Charlotte Brontë. She was his literary hero, but this regard paled on closer acquaintance for both parties.

This pencil traces *languishing* beauties, vacuous *languishing* vapid *languishing*

Lush of hair and rosy of skin with teeth which gleam and draw them in. Something infernal yet irresistible in these Ginevras and Paulinas which call siren to the hearts of men.

Languishing in tippet, waving billet doux, forsoothe, I mock and sneer but my own heart has been sunk, burnt Portsmouth figurehead effigy into Gallic waters, Literary waters, Emmanuel and George, running oil and salt, whiskers and diction.

Only my scarab-slicing words keep you up at night with taper and whiskey

Hard to put aside, sleepless nights...

But when you see my face, twisted carapace, I drown in shame because you frown involuntarily

you all frown

all of you frown

and I tuck my glazed heart away

The Meeting of the Waters

—This name was given to a local waterfall where the sisters used to meet and spend time together. It is now known as the Brontë waterfall.

Our waters run,

coupled,

sinuous through clagged brackish heath & chiff chaff overture,

There is no cure for teeming words which

spill lexical from our bitter cups which have seen

enough of this Haworth summer and

alight egret on expensive pages of bark which launch

our thoughts outside time.

Can you hear us, shivering in this scarred dell where waters gargle

midstream,

swifts dart,

turf leans into marine fossils

which chalk our fingers and lime our papercuts.

So slight we fold into an unpicked seam of history, but our books lay out our

paving.

Feel us here under embroidered canvas,

mudlark and holy,

A sister's morass of

clenched moulding

Héger

—Inspired by Charlotte Brontë's doomed infatuation with Monsieur Héger, her Master in The Pensionnat in Brussels where she was first a star pupil then a junior teacher.

His virility curled a page in me, wasted sensation when his dew was spent lavishly in the echoing chimera of Zoe Héger who knew enough to tack my longing back up in clinical white stitches   hissed together, malign and definite for my future humiliation.

What was there was not a lot to most, an obscure master fond of cigars and fencing rhetoric,

His schtick   to prick you 'til tears tumbled, then tame and titillate with a silent nosegay of profound apologies 'til striken   he held you charmed and aghast.

Old student in faded apparel, to this he cared not, but each new child a briar in my side as proof of a relentless passion I could easily have swallowed between husks of morose railings which impaled me to duty and musings hollow.

The distance to me seemed ribboned; a rosette of promise, my hopes relentless until the dawning then warning of the little wife.

She saw   she saw and warned, his ink dried, I scrunched a few words, balled in a fist, hurled into the wainscoting then recovered in brown atramentum, a queer pot pourri of flakes

he once breathed on.

Barège

—*Inspired by Charlotte Brontë's barège dress, archived and re-imagined by Dr Eleanor Hughton for The Brontë Parsonage Museum's 2022 exhibition, 'Defying Expectations: Inside Charlotte Brontë's Wardrobe'.*

— *"It is a solemn and strange and perilous thing for a woman to become a wife" Charlotte Brontë, 9 August 1854, LCB to EN*

Bradford French barège, drab as cured ham with a palsied spot, voluminous of sleeve and see-through scandalous, served up, unsullied to be curated by the curate who trembles at my look.

He'll take my gloved hand and kiss the gathered cuff with hook and eye.

The rest I'll draw a veil over except to sigh and murmur obliquely, a wife's lot is a solemn and perilous business, the trousseau just fancy packaging.

Handkerchief

—Inspired by Anne Brontë's futile journey to Scarborough to see the sea and take the air whilst dying of pulmonary tuberculosis. The sight of her blood-flecked handkerchief in the Brontë Parsonage Museum is a poignant one.

Crushed redcurrants splashed in a razor across my wakeful mind.

Scarborough waves crashed & sucked the coastline in ruched folds towards my skin.

Mother's snuff bottle clasped, a sharpener to my resolve.

Travel stagecoach 'cross brough & pastureland, let this ague dissolve into saline waters.

A bolt of cloth catch a seagull's cry, claret clarion gnaw 'neath silk

Automaton

Squeeze me tight persimmon fruit remove my soul from stultifying wood, flaking paint and squeaking castors.

Wheeled out to nod, smile, and say yes; be enchanting, scintillating, a

wit in these close saloons where eyes bore holes into my faded apparel.

Squeeze me until the marrow pops out, the juice, the ungodly, the uncommon, you'll have to squeeze as I'm trapped in this December doll, an automaton, the one with hair piece, invited to London to be titivated and courted.

Naturally I stink from travel and shrink to a tight hawthorn bud grown rotten with thought and choler. The

cost of fame is malcontent; I'll circumvent exposure, though I

gaze out through plastic eyes, the cogs still burn within

Charlotte Brontë's Striped Dress

How many shades of blue did you pale to on this reluctant frame?

Hair

—Inspired by a necklace made from Emily Brontë's long dark hair donated to The Brontë Society in 1950

She wound tentacles around us,

plaited long brown hair,

a coiled serpent you now cannot touch,

glassed in its lair of frozen artefacts,

clasped from a servant's care.

What's more, she should have been a general to an army,

such taciturn power,

her dharma was to stride and write the moor until

the wyld things descended, hawk and beast tamed her to something
fitting human company.

But now, the hordes gaze through glass at this remnant from an
impenetrable head

which said all it could in verse and prose.

The Impressions They Made
>   *—after the Brontë sisters*

it teased; the brush of much-mended cotton 'cross *molinia caerulea*

underskirts hung low courting bilberry paths, silken darned mourning
shoes over damp grass

blanket bog fired three crowberries from shark metal cannon,
variegated A, E, & C

whose fingers strung a wavy hair lass into tiny notes

oblique symphony tombed in beeswax

their sheaves of writings, a motte drawn from the mudraz of women's
history

hear whinchat and ring ouzel garland the skies with finer sound, gaelic
and yorkshire chit

chat on soft rush. a yen for the unspeakable

cankerous hankering boring holes in desks and tests of a teacher's
resolve

transcendentalist dreamers tipped a clutter of quill cutters and dip pens into marsh glen

wend their sampler, quilted truths pinned ruefully to the bannerol of liberty

Notes on Previous Publications and Research

'Oafs & Asses' first published in *West Trestle Review*, November/December 2022

'Enigma' first published in *Last Stanza Poetry Journal* January 2023

The author has express permission from Sassy Holmes, Programme Officer and Ann Dinsdale, chief curator of the Brontë Parsonage Museum to make reference to both public and private collections throughout this collection.

The author had a micro- residency producing a suite of Brontë themed wellbeing resources for The Brontë Society, Haworth, West Yorkshire, England in Summer 2022

References
—By Poem—

Rupture: Remembering the 1824 Crow Hill Bog Burst: Patrick Brontë as a Science Writer, Shawna Ross, pages 228-240, Brontë Studies: The Journal of the Brontë Society, Volume 46, 2021-Issue 3, published online June 28, 2021

The Lady Saved from the Waves: *'One black day my father burnt them because they contained foolish love-stories'.* LCB Vol 1 1829-1847 ed. Margaret Smith (Oxford: Clarendon Press, 1995), p.240

Homely: *"Homely-faced creature! She wants some Tomkins or another to love her and be in love with"* William Makepeace Thackeray, The Letters and Private Papers of William Makepeace Thackeray, Gordon N. Ray ed. London: Oxford University Press, 1945-46

Barège: *CB 'It is a solemn and strange and perilous thing for a woman to become a wife'* August 1854, Letter from CB to EN, Ashley MS 2452, British Library

Select Bibliography

Ann Dinsdale, *The Brontës at Haworth* (Francis Lincoln Ltd, 2006)

Ann Dinsdale, Sarah Laycock, Julie Akhurst *Brontë Relics: A Collection History* (The Brontë Society, 2012)

Eddie Flintoff, *In the Steps of The Brontës* (Countryside Books, 1993)

Claire Harman, *Charlotte Brontë: A Life* (Penguin Books, 2015)

Tom Howard, *Brontë Country*, (Grange Books, 1995)

Katherine Frank, *A Chainless Soul: A Life of Emily Brontë* (Boston, 1990)

Rebecca Fraser, *Charlotte Brontë,* (Vintage, 2003)

Lyndall Gordon, *Charlotte Brontë: A Passionate Life* (Vintage, 1995)

Daphne du Maurier, *The Infernal World of Branwell Brontë* (Penguin Classics, 1972)

Michael Stewart, *Walking the Invisible* (HQ, 2021)

Steven Wood, *Haworth* (Tempus, 2005)

Sharon Wright, *The Mother of the Brontës* (Pen and Sword Books Ltd, 2019)

Milton Keynes UK
Ingram Content Group UK Ltd.
UKHW012200220923
429169UK00004B/28